I0390730

Common-Sense Morality and the Moral-Maximum Profit Threshold

Becoming a Better People

By
Anthony Ferraioli, M.D.
Foreword by Jesse Ferraioli
Illustrated by Chip Ferraioli

Dedicated to becoming a better people.

Contents

FOREWORD

As I have grown into my teen years, dinner table discussions with my family have often consisted of topics like the gradual disintegration of common-sense morality in America and in American capitalism.

I have grown up spewing out phrases such as 'superficial culture of impulsivity', and, 'Malignant Capitalism ultimately kills the host like an unchecked cancer'--along with my personal favorite, 'best to live deliberately, not reactively'.

As one might expect, a sophomore in high school is easily shaped by discussions such as these.

I have lived my life to this point with eyes wide open, refusing to succumb to what my dad would call "mediocrity" in depth of thought or analysis.

I have been fed reality and moral lessons at that dinner table and they have influenced how I both perceive and react to situations, especially in terms of the pursuit of true quality and excellence versus the cutting of corners and the taking of shortcuts.

A few months back, I was working on a group project in school. The goal was to fabricate a machine that could put together three blocks in a certain way--then repeat this five times.

This machine had to be produced at the lowest possible cost while still being able to put the blocks together at the fastest possible rate--and the highest grade would be awarded to the group that created the most "efficient" machine.

Two weeks into the project, and we were down to the final few days.

Our group was neck-and-neck with another, vying for first place. Both groups' machines were by now reduced to the minimum number of pieces in order to lower production cost as much as possible while still allowing a degree of functionality.

The way it went was that, by this time, THE BLOCKS WERE NO LONGER EVEN BEING ASSEMBLED CORRECTLY EACH TIME--and yet this was allowed because BOTH machines that were leading the "competition" were performing like this.

The message was that it was no longer truly about quality of product, but, instead, about time--and therefore--bottom-line profit above all else, including the actual product being produced.

In the end, my group lost by three seconds.

However, the project had set off all sorts of red flags in my 15-year-old mind: themes related to the concepts of Malignant Capitalism and Moral Maximums that were discussed at our dinner table at home.

I had now experienced the loss of substance, quality, and common-sense morality that I had been taught to value at that table; all given up as a sacrifice to the bottom-line, which, in this case, was a grade in school--but could very well have been money.

This project brought home to me the valuable lesson my father gives in this short book; that in the end, ignoring the Moral Maximum threshold amounts to also disregarding true innovation, and it leads to a shift towards amoral and destructive work habits and production.

In the case of the above vignette, only a grade was at stake.

Applied to a larger scale, we have a destructive epidemic of substance-loss and greed on our hands.

We no longer have competition for excellence and real innovation, but only the cold, hard, bottom-line. The resulting product may not be better (in fact, it may well be quite a bit worse), but it WILL make more money, and that's all we care about.

Cost-cutting and mediocrity above the pursuit of excellence.

Not good.

I hope you let this short book be to you what our dinner table discussions were/are to me.

Jesse Ferraioli
Thanksgiving Day 2016

THE MORAL MAXIMUM

The Moral Maximum is the Maximum Profit that can be gotten out of a product or service AND from the people providing them before the quality of that product or service begins to decline OR the worker's rewards begin to decrease.

Once it crosses over the Moral Maximum, an organization becomes Malignant, meaning it is no longer innovating to create continued profits, only cost-cutting both its product and its people.***[1]

Another word for Malignant is greedy.

---

[1] ***see Figures 1-3

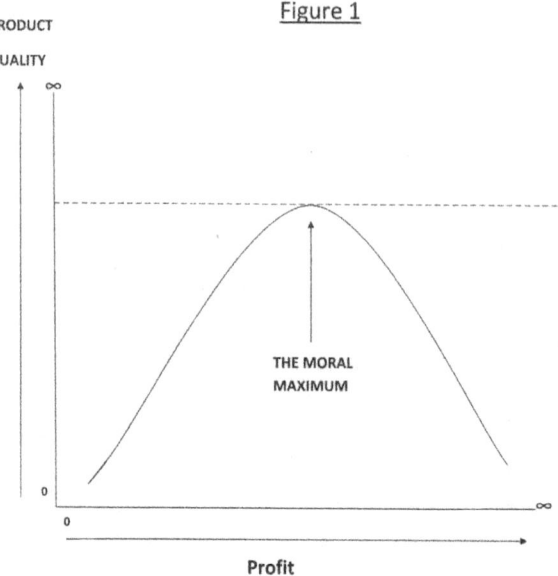

PRODUCT

QUALITY

Figure 1

THE MORAL
MAXIMUM

Profit

MORAL MAXIMUM= Point on curve where profit is maximized
while product quality and worker compensation ALSO
maximized.

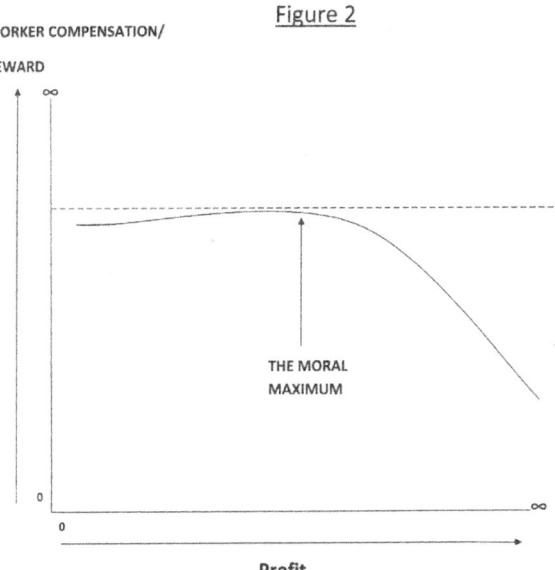

Figure 2

MORAL MAXIMUM= Point on curve where profit is maximized while product quality and worker compensation ALSO maximized.

Figure 3

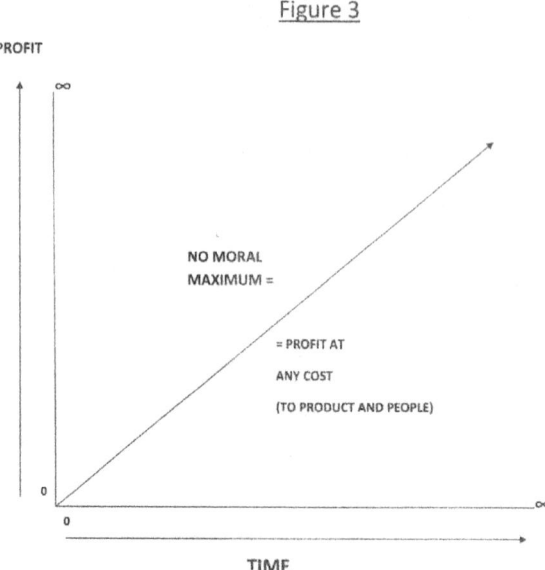

AS PROFIT APPROACHES INFINITY, PRODUCT QUALITY APPROACHES ZERO

AS PROFIT APPROACHES INFINITY, WORKER COMPENSATION APPROACHES ZERO

MALIGNANT

If the trend into Malignancy continues, regarding either the cutting of the quality of product or service OR the continuous cutting of the rewards of the people providing them, the providers of said products or services will eventually succumb to a state of merely trying to survive financially--resulting in a shift in focus from providing excellence in the quality of their product or service, to a singular focus on their own economic survival and security.

The result is an ever-increasingly poor quality product or service, coupled with an ever-decreasingly secure and motivated workforce--along with the cessation of the kind of real, long-term economic growth that can only be had through continuous innovation and competition, not endless cost-cutting and oppression of the makers, producers, and innovators.

Crossing over the Moral Maximum profit threshold is a counterproductive and destructive extreme that can occur at both ends of the spectrum of economic systems--at the one extreme by the tendency towards greed in a free market, competitive system, and at the other by socialistic or noncompetitive-type systems such as pure socialism or communism.

These two extremes in economic systems help illustrate how an organization can get to the same endpoint in terms of minimal quality of products or services produced under very different economic systems; that is, in both systems, quality and excellence ultimately become no longer of central concern when compared to the worker's basic economic survival.

In summary, as an organization continues to push profits past the Moral Maximum profit threshold in order to get to the absolute maximum profit level, there is a shift in the worker's focus from quality and excellence of product and service to their own basic economic security and survival.

This is a shift towards self-preservation and away from creative, generative, competitive productivity.

In the case of competitive, free-market systems, this shift occurs because of long-term psychological changes towards mere survival mode in human beings exposed to the endless greed of organizations without Moral Maximum profit thresholds.

Interestingly, these changes would be similar or perhaps even identical to those one might observe in the opposite sort of economic system: i.e., non-competitive systems like communism.

How might we further describe these psychological changes and why are they bad for business over the long haul, including for sustainable profit growth?

To start, hopelessness sets in as baser level, reactive brain functions designed for survival kick in and take over.

Survival instincts begin to override thoughtful, forebrain-based cognitive and emotional processes such as the processing of consequences for actions and the modulation of impulsivity, rage, and extreme despair.

Ultimately, in the extreme, there is a shift towards increased, widespread systemic micro- and gross-violence towards both self and others, as socially acceptable, adult-emotionally-competent behaviors give way to brute force and a reactive, reflexive mentality.

Without a Moral Maximum, the people producing the ever decreasing-in-real-value products and services ultimately come to be minimized in value themselves--as their monetary and security rewards are continuously minimized by the organizations or industries in which they work, in order for profits to be continuously maximized without limit.

The worker is ultimately left hopeless, unmotivated, and demoralized.

Carelessness, indifference, and complacency eventually ensue, along with accompanying shifts in both physical and mental health.

In the extreme, there is an eventual, gradual shift towards amoral or even overtly immoral and self-destructive work habits and values, as life itself becomes but a hopeless challenge to be merely survived; a living hell on earth of financial slavery and indentured servitude.

Not exactly good for morale.

Nor for innovation and excellence.

Don't believe me? Ask any doctor what it's been like to practice medicine over the past twenty years or so, and you'll hear all about it.

You'll hear how they--and their patients--are suffering, as the quality of the services they're allowed by their owners and handlers to provide has become mortally wounded and devalued while at the same time their overall workloads have gone up, factory-style, in order to feed the unquenchable and unlimited profit-hunger of the industries that own them and their practices.

The quality of services provided is continuously minimized.

The value and monetary security of doctors and other healthcare providers is continuously minimized.

And, with this, the current, sorry state of the quality of healthcare delivery is explained.

That there are entire industries (healthcare being just one of them) where the Moral Maximum profit threshold is not only ignored, but where it has been ignored for decades, has become de rigueur.

And left behind in this mass cheapening and devaluing of products and people are the empty shells of what was; i.e. of the former levels of quality and value of products and services in these industries, along with those of their providers.

We are left with what might be called "survival chaos", which goes along with a lack of any true innovation, creativity, or real worker commitment in these fields, and, finally, by the cost-cutting technique of the hiring of nothing more than the minimum number of warm bodies needed--regardless of credentials--to keep these organizations afloat as empty profit makers and money producers for their owners.

The aforementioned state of relentlessly and systematically diminishing the real value or worth of products and services, and the people providing them, eventually leads to a state of unhealthy capitalism that my co-author and I called in a previous book--one by the same name--"Malignant Capitalism"; which, in short, means greed.

Thus the concept of the Moral Maximum profit threshold is designed to help organizations maintain and grow profits, while, at the same time, decreasing the risk of turning Malignant.

As my co-author and I explained in that book, Malignant Capitalism is the opposite of healthy, competitive, free-market capitalism mainly in that it does not promote innovation and competition.

In fact, it promotes just the opposite.

Malignant Capitalism--by ignoring the idea of a Moral Maximum profit threshold designed to keep both product and people fresh and motivated--hamstrings itself and makes itself unsustainable in the long run.

Another theme in that book worth repeating here is that Malignant Capitalism stupidly extinguishes itself in much the same way that unchecked cancer does in the human body: by ultimately killing the host.

Given that, we might consider the notion or metric of a Moral Maximum profit threshold to be like chemotherapy for Malignant Capitalism, in that it challenges organizations to examine and to consider not just the most absolute, bottom-line profitable way to do business, but, instead, the most balanced, most sustainable, and most morally upright way to do business.

The Moral Maximum doesn't just ask, "Will we make more money?", but also, "Is this the BEST way we can make more money?"

And perhaps, ultimately, the introduction of a Moral Maximum will allow organizations the chance to ask themselves who they really are, what sort of people they want to attract, and what they really want to stand for. We used to call this reputation.

This is good for business, because it promotes a fresh, growth-sustaining edge in an organization.

It promotes a deeper reflection and focus on the business at hand--as well as real innovation--as opposed to the relentless, ongoing cost-cutting of product and people.

And it also prevents the fear-based survival mode and stagnation that leads to the unhealthy, Malignant conversion of an organization.

With the Moral Maximum, if an organization wants to continue to stay profitable and fit, it must find better ways to innovate and to do business than just simple, continuous cost-cutting.

You cross the Moral Maximum profit threshold when you cheapen a product in order to make more money.

You cross the Moral Maximum profit threshold when you abuse the makers and the providers of your products and services in order to make more money.

The Moral Maximum promotes healthy, strong, free-market competition and capitalism by promoting the innovation and creativity which have always been at the core of real, true progress in any industry or endeavor--and by which we can continuously fuel our hopes not only for doing better business, but for creating a better people and a better world.

The Moral Maximum promotes that which is productive rather than destructive; it promotes that which is sustainable and growth-producing rather than self-limiting and stagnant.

And, by promoting innovation and creativity instead of morally lazy and destructive cost-cutting and devaluing of products, services, and people, the Moral Maximum decreases or eliminates entirely the demoralization and paralysis of the worker by encouraging the full expression of his or her knowledge, natural talents, and experience with rewards instead of punishment.

Ultimately, in just one phrase, here's what we stand to gain:

We'll start caring again.

Doctors will be allowed to be doctors again.

Nurses will be allowed to be nurses again.

Teachers will be allowed to teach again.

Information technology professionals, customer services providers, cooks, chefs, journalists, etc.--they will be allowed to be driven by the motivation to perfect their skills, rather than by the fear of financial and professional extinction.

With the introduction of the Moral Maximum to an organization's business model you eliminate the objectification and continuous devaluing of the worker--and you get a more motivated, happier, healthier workforce.

Work becomes sustenance--both financial and otherwise.

People will no longer need to numb themselves up with bad lifestyle habits and choices in order to deal with the continuous pain of living on an arbitrary chopping block that has almost nothing to do with how good (or not good) they are at what they do.

People will live better and will be happier, healthier.

Healthcare costs will go down, naturally.

And you will have generations of people who actually WANT to learn and to become competent in their chosen fields; people who want to be the very best they can be at what they do.

These are the people who will help innovate and build; they will think, perform, and serve with pride and with purpose.

Honest, morally sound profits will be earned and people and organizations will still become wealthy--the right way.

Careers will once again become something to be proud of and something to nurture; they will matter and they will exist for the long-term as something to invest in and to shape.

Real mentoring will exist again.

Work, creating, and contributing will sustain us rather than demoralize and enslave us, and our work lives will no longer trigger mere survival instincts in us.

With the Moral Maximum profit threshold, products and services--as well as the people providing them--will have real value and real pride invested in them.

The optimism and freedom of possibility-thinking and imagining will replace stale cynicism and hopelessness.

Playfulness, creativity, and whole-hearted dedication will re-enter the work realm and replace trauma and sheer survival mode; and the economy will benefit from the culling of the best of our human nature, rather than the worst.

With the Moral Maximum, people can be real, whole people again: engaged, interested, proud, balanced, and fulfilled--rather than simple, robotic drones who are dead inside.

There will be an end to the morbid lifestyle of just getting by and cruising along numbly until the next weekend, holiday, retirement, and, eventually, death.

And we will live again.

And we will become a better people.

JUST BECAUSE YOU CAN DOESN'T MEAN YOU SHOULD

We have become ugly.

Whenever you care more about the bottom-line than anything else, you become ugly.

And part of the reason we have become so ugly is that we have become increasingly more efficiency-based and efficacy-based than we are morally-based.

It no longer matters if something is right or wrong, as long as it works:

As long as it makes us money.

As long as it wins the fight.

As long as it shuts the other person up.

Whatever it is, we look for the easy way, not the right way.

We look for the highest profits.

We look for the quickest way to shut the other person's argument down.

We don't think long-term, only short-term.

We do it in parenting, in marriage, and in business.

We do it in our professions, and we do it in our friendships.

We have become moral cowards.

Compassion and thoughtfulness has been replaced by the hard, cold bottom-line.

We have forgotten that kindness comes from strength and security, not from weakness, threat, and insecurity.

We falsely believe that we cannot have both compassion AND excellence, so we live our lives by the false dichotomy that you have to choose between the two.

And that's wrong.

There's a slippery slope between being "hard-nosed" and being amoral, or immoral.

Kids are educated, but not morally educated, so they go out and eat each other for breakfast: ever-smiling, but merciless and without compassion.

They are taught spin rather than substance; hand-waving rather than deep thought.

Superficial.

Inhuman.

Inhumane.

Morality is quickly equated with and dismissed as a sort of subtopic of human sexuality, resulting in lost opportunities for broad discussion and thought about right and wrong outside of sexual subject matter.

Taboo.

Unwelcome.

Don't talk about it.

Common-Sense Morality has nothing to do with sex or sexuality; it's about not stabbing your fellow human in the back:

It's about not being careless with your power over others, no matter how much or how little.

It's about being humble enough to reflect upon your own shortcomings and the possibility that you might be wrong about something or someone.

It's about being deliberate rather than reactive in your life.

And none of the above threatens you with having to become a stilted, rehearsed, passionless, soulless robot.

Just the opposite is true.

You can be just as passionate and unique as you are or want to be and still become a better, more morally upright human being.

Because, remember, no matter what your talents and passions, you will also need a degree of virtue in order to fulfill those talents and passions to their greatest potential:

A degree of patience.

A degree of humility and healthy self-doubt.

A degree of self-reflection.

A degree of commitment.

And a degree of moral courage that enables you to "go there."

It's really up to you.

You can settle for mediocrity, like so many do in today's automaton world.

Or you can really excel as a human being and experience true joy.

You can just do the minimal; i.e., what you HAVE to do.

Or you can truly live.

HUMILITY AND SOME HEALTHY SELF-DOUBT

Why do you feel threatened by the thought of not being right?

Whatever happened to having an attitude of exploration and learning, rather than one of being right vs. wrong?

And why don't we start every disagreement with the thought of where we ourselves might be wrong?

Imagine that? Or perhaps with how or what we might not fully understand?

What's with all the morally weak, prideful bravado and defensiveness?

Are we not adults?

Why are self-questioning and humility seen as weaknesses?

And why is blind self-assuredness and outward aggression seen as strength?

It's all backwards.

Great leaders are borne of honest self-evaluation and courageous strengthening of weak-points, not of instantaneous assumption or presumption of one's own greatness.

That's just weakness in disguise.

And you can't trust a weak leader or you'll eventually get stabbed in the back;

In your business.

In your family.

In the leadership above you, generally.

And the surest mark of weak leaders, whether they be in your family or at your job, is that they constantly claim outwardly, overtly to be strong.

Weak leaders create chaos, division, and infighting.

Strong leaders create order, unity, and safety for all.

They create peace.

INTELLECT ALONE VS. MORALLY-INFORMED INTELLECT

Anybody can be born with a high IQ.

And almost anybody, with enough hard work and dedication, can excel academically.

But just because you were the valedictorian of your class, does not automatically make you a boon to humankind.

In fact, you might be quite the opposite.

You may even be quite dangerous.

The world is full of people with powerful intellects and prestigious educations who remain unfettered by any sense of common-sense morality, and they can cause a lot of pain and misery for others.

And they have.

Without a moral compass, the honed intellect will choose what it thinks is the most effective or efficient solution to a problem--or the problem as defined by it--without concern for right or wrong:

And without common sense morality, that intellect can be quiet easily influenced by and primarily motivated by things like greed, self-promotion, and bottom-line thinking and reward seeking.

Here's the real bottom-line: education without moral education can--and has--produced some very powerful humans throughout history.

Human monsters, that is.

PATIENCE AND SACRIFICE

You cannot have patience without sacrifice--nor vice-versa.

When you practice being patient, you are sacrificing your impulses and your anxieties.

You are practicing impulse control and respect for others.

Leadership is another word for sacrifice.

You don't have to demand respect:

You earn respect by being the sacrifice.

At home.

At work.

In your community.

The leader is the sacrifice:

That means the parent, not the child.

The boss, not the employee.

The rich and powerful, not the poor and oppressed.

The officer, not the rank-and-file.

And we need to get this straight, once and for all.

Cultivating patience and sacrifice is at the heart of common-sense morality and it is at the heart of strong leadership.

COMMITMENT

What does the word mean to you?

What it should mean is that once you commit to something--unless there are extreme, unforeseeable, or unhealthy, destructive circumstances, (such as an abusive relationship)--you stay committed.

It means that you respect committing more than you respect quitting.

It means that you move on, past the "deciding to commit" phase, and into the next phase, where you dedicate your energies to fulfilling the commitment rather than endlessly deciding whether or not you are GOING to commit (which is the definition of non-committal).

It means that you don't run from the pain, fear, and consistency involved with following through with your commitment.

Commitment does NOT mean Convenience.

We don't commit, just for now.

When we don't commit to anything, we fail to honor the very pursuit of finding what's best in ourselves and in others.

Because we never get there.

Because we quit instead.

When we habitually break commitments that get too hard to keep, we lose respect.

And we lose self-respect.

And when we continuously fail to commit to anything, we never go deeper; we never learn to transcend the pain barrier and get to a new plateau.

You can't have healthy, secure relationships without commitment.

You can't have a truly rewarding, generative work life without commitment.

And, here's the rub:

You can't see your commitments through without first learning to deal with and to *heal from your emotional pain and your inner demons.*

What a bonus.

POLISHED VENEER VS. SUBSTANCE

The world doesn't need more spin-doctors.

You know, the people who can make anything sound good--or at least however they want it or need it to sound, regardless of the truth:

They juggle words and numbers, masterfully making them dance along to any beat that serves their purpose, whether good or bad.

What the world needs instead is more truth.

More substance.

More sincerity.

More authenticity.

We need thinkers and doers, not pretenders and posers.

We need people of honor and integrity, not empty shells hungry for our minds and our souls.

We need substance, not just style and strategy.

And we need more people who mean what they say and say what they mean, sincerely.

To this end, in some ways, language is most important, in other ways, maybe not so much.

Besides the words we use, tone can help differentiate between spin and substance, as can intentionality and agenda.

You can kid with a loved one and the choice of words may not matter much; with someone else, it may matter quite a lot.

But, most of all--and especially if I don't know you:

Before I will give any serious consideration to what you are saying to me or how you are saying it, I will want to know who you are.

I want to know how you live your life, what you've been through, and what you stand for.

In other words, I want to know your substance, not just your veneer.

THE MONEY MOTIVE: CONTINUOUS MONETIZATION

Ever notice the major modern theme, as reductionistic as it is real, of monetizing everything possible?

Have a talent? You can make money from it.

Have an idea? Money.

We have monetized human relationships and strife (reality TV), fear, disease, sports and other games, and even religion.

Sometimes we need to skip over monetization and just live.

It's called having a soul.

And we've lost our souls to the worship of money.

Yes, it is healthy and good to be productive and to get paid for your work.

But it is unhealthy and unbalanced to be constantly looking for opportunities to leverage everything--and everyone--into your pocket for your own financial gain.

It's one thing to take advantage of opportunities that present themselves to you.

And to even look for opportunities in areas that sincerely interest you and that allow to you make an honest contribution while enriching yourself financially and otherwise.

But it is quite another thing--an unhealthy, destructive thing--to constantly obsess about and endlessly focus upon the accumulation of money.

The constant search for opportunities to monetize things and people cannot help but turn you into an opportunist.

And it can't help but eventually pit you against your fellow human beings when it comes to making morally upright decisions while you are all the while trying to monetize them.

Opportunists don't live lives; they leverage other people's lives.

They are like soulless, modern day vampires--empty shells of human beings, constantly craving your life-blood, and hell to be around.

SELF-IMPOSED VICTIMHOOD

The world is full of actual victims.

Victims of assault.

Victims of abuse: physical, sexual, emotional, financial.

People's lives are full of trauma, both now and throughout the ages.

It's a miracle that we as individuals, we as a species, and we as a race--THE HUMAN RACE--have survived it all to get to the present day.

Given this backdrop of pain and victimization--of our consistent history of inhumanity to each other and carelessness with both ourselves and with our planet--we must conclude that we need to pull ourselves together and work on healing and getting stronger if we are to survive as a species.

To endlessly seek out differences and causes for division among ourselves is the same as seeking retribution: it only produces further division and trauma.

And it makes it easier for those who may seek to divide and to manipulate us with whatever sort of ill-intentioned agenda they may have--whether by the use of financial slavery, or by dumbing us down and numbing us up, or by physical violence--to gain control of us, to demoralize us, and to leverage us to their own selfish gain.

So be vigilant.

Tend to your wounds and to the wounds of your brothers and your sisters.

But do not insult one another.

Instead, seek to understand yourself and one another:

Seek to learn before you judge.

See each other and yourselves first and foremost as human beings--before you may or may not see other things that can be used to divide you:

Seek healing.

Seek knowledge.

Seek truth.

And be honorable. Not greedy. Not devious. And don't make your life all about leveraging others to your gain.

Because remember: if all you set forth to seek is victimhood, it will come all too easily.

REAL ADULTS

In the end, all we have to help us get stronger, to heal, and to become a better people is knowledge, faith, and our emotional competence as R.E.A.L.A.D.U.L.TS.:

R-estraint: take a moment to think before you act

E-ngagement: learn to feel joy and interest in your life

A-nger modulation: learn how to do it so it doesn't control you

L-iving with pain and failure: instead of acting it out

A-nxiety modulation: see anger modulation above

D-eliberate living: instead of reactive living

U-nconditional positive regard: give the benefit of the doubt; innocent before proven guilty

L-VAC: Listen, Validate, Ask, & Comment last (see my LVAC Nation book)

T-one: watch it

S-topping: learn how to be still with yourself, your thoughts, and your feelings